EXPERIENCE EXPLORER

From Yesterday's Lessons to Tomorrow's Success

About the Center for Creative Leadership

The Center for Creative Leadership (CCL) is a top-ranked global provider of leadership development. By leveraging the power of leadership to drive results that matter most to clients, CCL transforms individual leaders, teams, organizations, and society. Our array of cutting-edge solutions is steeped in extensive research and experience gained from working with hundreds of thousands of leaders at all levels. Ranked among the world's Top 5 providers of executive education by the *Financial Times* and in the Top 10 by *Bloomberg BusinessWeek*, CCL has offices in Greensboro, NC; Colorado Springs, CO; San Diego, CA; Brussels, Belgium; Moscow, Russia; Addis Ababa, Ethiopia; Johannesburg, South Africa; Singapore; Gurgaon, India; and Shanghai, China.

EXPERIENCE EXPLORER

*From Yesterday's Lessons
to Tomorrow's Success*

Facilitator's Guide

Meena S. Wilson and N. Anand Chandrasekar

CENTER FOR CREATIVE LEADERSHIP
www.ccl.org

CCL Stock No. PM012B
ISBN 978-1-60491-535-8
© 2014 Center for Creative Leadership

Published by CCL Press

Sylvester Taylor, Director of Assessments, Tools, and Publications
Peter Scisco, Manager, Publication Development
Stephen Rush, Editor
Shaun Martin, Associate Editor

Design and Layout by Joanne Ferguson

With Special Thanks

to our unflagging supporters for their zest, guidance, and diligence: David Altman, Kathryn Brendon, Michael Campbell, Corey Criswell, Amit Desai, Karen Dyer, George Hallenbeck, Emily Hoole, David Horth, Renee Hultin, V. Kartikeyan, Jennifer Martineau, Cindy McCauley, Chuck Palus, Peter Scisco, Anupam Sirbhaiya, Pankaj Sethi, Clemson Turregano, Ellen Van Velsor, and Marie Van Vuren;

to our prototype makers: Oliver Bermoy and Michelle Crouch;

to our early adopters: Vered Asif, Al Calarco, Steadman Harrison, Paula Nielsen-Lazo, Nicholas Petrie, Tzipi Radonsky, Lyndon Rego, Philomena Rego, and Lim Peng Soon;

and to our many research partners, including Tata Management Training Centre in India, Civil Service College in Singapore, and China Europe International Business School in India.

Without the efforts of these people and organizations, making Experience Explorer would not have been possible.

Quick Guide

Experience Explorer enhances the lessons of experience by giving leaders a simple, energizing way to share stories that advance their development. A typical Experience Explorer session lasts one to three hours and follows four steps.

LESSONS LESSONS

1. Set Objectives
Outline clear objectives for the session and communicate these to the participants.

2. Sort and Select
Guide participants to sort the cards and to select experiences that have affected their leadership development or to choose leadership lessons that reflect current strengths or capabilities necessary for future success.

EXPERIENCE

4. Strategize
Guide participants to create plans to improve their leadership effectiveness.

3. Share
Create conditions for sharing of memories and insights about the selected experiences or lessons, so that participants may learn from each other and the facilitator.

LESSONS LESSONS

Contents

Introduction

Leadership development is driven by experience; in other words, leaders learn not just through training and developmental relationships but through job and leadership experiences. In training-and-development circles and among human-resources staff, the catchphrase "70-20-10" is a general guideline for combining challenging assignments (70%), developmental relationships (20%), and coursework & training (10%). This guideline suggests that a combination of those learning opportunities, at about that ratio, is optimal for preparing managers for leadership roles. The 70-20-10 ratio should not be taken as a one-size-fits-all solution to developing leaders. However, the pattern that 70-20-10 suggests is clear: On-the-job experiences are a significant driver of leadership development, particularly experiences that challenge leaders to lead in novel and diverse environments.

Beyond 70-20-10

Research by the Center for Creative Leadership (CCL) has identified two other categories of developmental experiences important for leaders: hardships and personal life experiences. Hardships are not included in the 70-20-10 guideline because these are not experiences that organizations intentionally give individuals for development; personal life experiences are not included because they are outside of an organization's control.

Experience Explorer gives leaders a powerful and efficient tool for discovering what they have learned about effective leadership and what they still need to learn. When leaders explore and talk about their past experiences, they can better plan future learning experiences.

Leaders and managers at all organizational levels and in all types of organizations are typically responsible for developing themselves and others. Whether they work in human resources, serve as training-and-development consultants, or lead a business unit, managers and leaders can use Experience Explorer in a number of situations.

Leading an Experience Explorer session does not require high-level facilitation skills. The 99 cards in the package are divided into 52 blue Experience cards, 42 orange Lesson cards, and 5 white Instruction cards. The Instruction cards can be used when this facilitator's guide is unavailable or is not needed.

Did You Know?

In the first study from which the 70-20-10 guideline originated, 189 of 191 participating executives were men! To learn about women's experiences and lessons, CCL conducted a follow-on study of 76 executive women and found a development ratio of 55-40-5. The issue of why women report less development through challenging assignments and greater development due to developmental relationships continues to raise questions: Are women given far fewer opportunities to meet business challenges?

Experience Explorer is based on 40 years of international research that CCL has conducted in several countries from various regions of the world. The tool's Experience and Lesson cards are derived from a comprehensive inventory of essential experiences and lessons as described to researchers by successful leaders. People of all ages and of different countries and various walks of life have found that the experiences and lessons described in the cards capture much of the know-how they have built up during their careers.

However, Experience Explorer is much more than a personal inventory of experiences and lessons. It emphasizes the specific findings at the core of CCL's Lessons of Experience research. Those studies show that there are fifteen types of experiences and three dimensions of lessons common to leading in organizations. Experience Explorer represents those experiences and dimensions with symbols that are illustrated in Table 1 and that appear on the Experience Explorer cards (Figures 1 and 2).

In addition to those symbols, each Experience card is marked with a colored dot in the lower-right corner (Figure 1). The dots map to the guideline of 70-20-10. Turn to the Options and Applications section for ideas about using the dots or three dimensions of lessons during an Experience Explorer session.

Table 1. Fifteen core leadership experiences and their Experience Explorer symbols

	EXPERIENCE	DESCRIPTION
	Bosses & Superiors	You interacted with a leader one or more levels above you, and you remember that leader as a positive or as a negative role model, coach, teacher, or catalyst who accelerated your development.
	Career Setback	You experienced an unforeseen and unwanted block to your career progression, caused by another person or event—for example, being fired, demoted, passed over for promotion, or placed in a job that did not match your skills, aptitude, or knowledge.
	Coursework & Training	You chose, or your organization sponsored you, to attend a development-and-training class that advanced your learning, growth, or career progress.
	Crisis	You experienced an unexpected, shocking event that you could not fully control and that caused feelings of confusion or loss. Typically, the disorder that follows a crisis brings unfavorable publicity to an organization, threatens the reputation and survival of top leaders and the organization, or injures individual, organizational, and even national interests. Examples include a product recall, an investigation into ethics violations, a personal scandal, a natural disaster, or a health epidemic.
	Cultural Crossing	You had regular, direct contact with coworkers whose values, motivations, language, life routines, and social customs are different from yours. Your organization may have relocated you to another region or country with different political, economic, and legal systems from your home area.
	Difficult People	You worked with a boss, subordinates, or peers who provoked tension, resentment, and disputes due to differing working styles, preferences, and opinions. The resulting situations—which you or they may not always have handled skillfully—could have involved feelings of ineptness, confrontation, excessive competition, jealousy, or betrayal.
	Ethical Dilemma	You observed fraudulent, illegal, or immoral behavior by a senior leader that was endured by a lower-level manager or directed toward you.
	Feedback & Coaching	You have had job-related, formal or informal conversations concerning specific situations or personal abilities or traits, or you received advice about leading or managing. The feedback and coaching may or may not have been part of a formal performance-appraisal or 360-degree-feedback process or mentoring program.

Table 1. Fifteen core leadership experiences and their Experience Explorer symbols (cont.)

	EXPERIENCE	DESCRIPTION
	Horizontal Move	You transitioned or were rotated into another function, business unit, organization, or industry sector where the work and work culture were different from what you were used to. The move did not involve a promotion and was initiated either by yourself or by your organization.
	Increase in Job Scope	You experienced a significant increase in budget, in the number of people you managed, in access to resources, and in complexity of tasks. These changes typically involved a promotion, an increase in job scope, and an expansion of management responsibilities and visibility.
	Mistake	You experienced an error of judgment by a manager or by coworkers that resulted in a team's or the organization's failure to meet its goals. Such mistakes can be technical, professional, ethical, or strategic—for example, a product malfunction, a poor hiring decision, a loss of credibility or face, or a collapsed venture.
	New Initiative	You built something by leveraging an opportunity to develop or launch a new product or service, to adopt new technologies, to craft a new policy or process, to set up a plant or unit, to enter a new market, to embark on a new line of business, or to create a new business.
	Personal Experience	You have emotion-laden memories of times in your life when you formed values, sorted out your approach to challenges, or set out on a different direction. Such experiences influence a person's principles, attitudes, and behaviors. Examples include incidents in early life, youth leadership roles, family situations, early job experiences, spiritual encounters, personal traumas, and mid-life transitions.
	Stakeholder Engagement	You experienced high-level interactions, typically with people outside of your organization, that called for reconciling competing points of view and working out solutions when you had little or no formal authority. Stakeholder engagements can produce controversy or feelings of failure.
	Turnaround/ Fix-it	You fixed or stabilized a failing or underperforming business unit or organization. During the process, you achieved an increase in productivity and profitability by restructuring; downsizing; closing the unit, function, or operation; or implementing an organizational culture change. These kinds of assignments often arouse turbulent thoughts and feelings.

Figure 1. Experience card

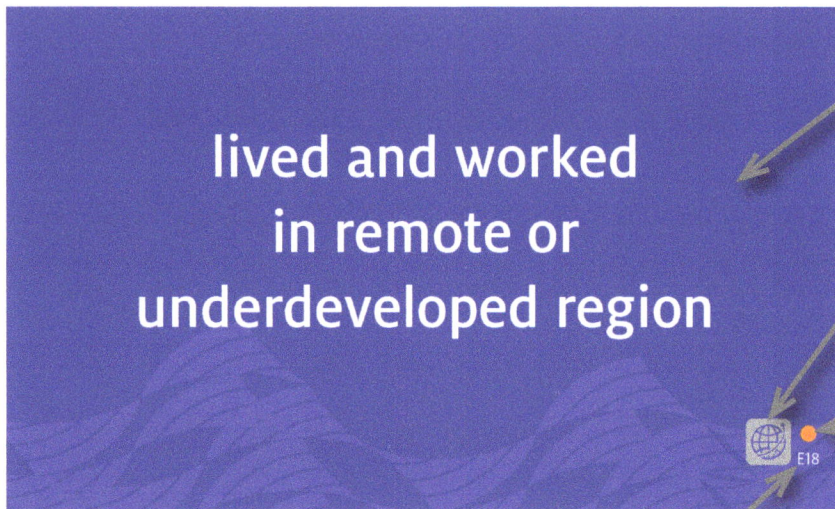

lived and worked
in remote or
underdeveloped region

E18

The card describes a common managerial or leadership experience.

This symbol represents one of the fifteen key experience types.

Colored dots indicate whether this experience stems from:
- a challenging assignment,
- a developmental relationship,
- coursework & training,
- a hardship, or
- a personal life experience.

An "E" marks this as an Experience card and the number indicates which of the 52 cards it is.

Figure 2. Lesson card

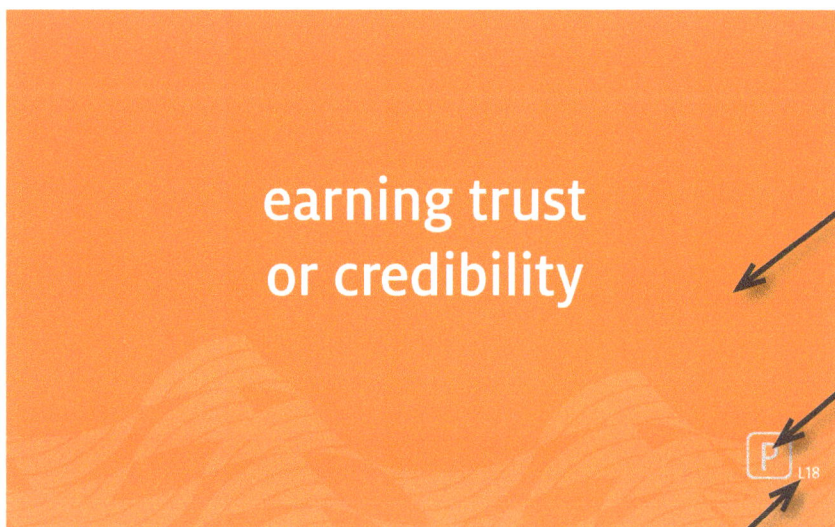

earning trust
or credibility

P L18

The card describes a lesson associated with managerial or leadership experiences.

The leadership dimension in which the lesson can be applied (work, people, self).

An "L" marks this as a Lesson card and the number indicates which of the 42 cards it is.

Important Experiences

The Lessons of Experience research has found that these five experiences teach approximately 55% of all leadership lessons:

- Bosses & Superiors
- Turnaround
- Increase in Job Scope
- Horizontal Move
- New Initiative

Figure 3. You can use Experience Explorer for self-reflection, in one-on-one sessions, or with small or large groups.

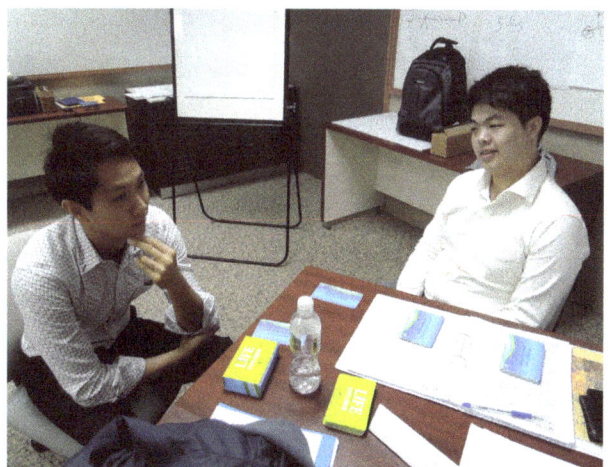

Using Experience Explorer

Experience Explorer can be used in any number of ways and with all kinds of people. Most commonly, groups of leaders have used it to talk about their work and life experiences, to gain insights about how to develop themselves and others, and to map out their future development. In practice, there are few limits to the tool's use.

It works with groups of almost any size. A leader can use it alone for self-reflection. As a one-on-one coaching tool, Experience Explorer can work as a conversation starter and help people develop a rapport so that they can more fully share their lessons of experience, including the emotional impact. It can help small groups engage in and support developmental conversations in settings such as breakout groups at a conference or during training sessions. It has also been used successfully as a networking activity with large groups.

You can use Experience Explorer with almost any type of audience and in various institutional settings, including public and private businesses, government agencies, nonprofit organizations, and educational units. It works across organizational departments and functions, such as finance, human resources, operations, research and development, sales, and marketing, and with people in various professions and at different levels in the same organization. Graduate and undergraduate students can also benefit from using Experience Explorer because it can help them validate some of their experiences and anticipate what they will face once they join an organization. Younger students at school and in extracurricular programs, camps, and retreats can use it to identify, share, and learn from each other's experiences. The purpose for using the tool doesn't have to be explicitly related to leadership. For a younger group, an activity might deal with what they have learned about working with others or about what their experiences say about themselves.

How Does It Work?

The core issue that Experience Explorer tackles is profoundly simple: How can leaders and managers make learning from their experiences *intentional*, not incidental or accidental?

During a session, the cards encourage participants to remember and reflect on experiences they have had during their careers and what they have learned from those experiences.

As leaders reflect on and share their most pivotal incidents, events, and encounters, they uncover the lessons that they have learned and used. As they listen to others share their experiences, leaders see how varied experiences lead to many different lessons. The insights they gain from the session can be shared with others and used immediately, or used to plan the developmental experiences they need to broaden and deepen their capacity to lead. Simply put, Experience Explorer validates and reinforces lessons learned from experiences.

There are many ways in which leaders can benefit from using Experience Explorer. For instance, they can

- assist others to map their career journeys

- quickly identify their leadership strengths and gaps

- help generate profiles of the capabilities necessary to succeed in different roles and functions in their organizations

- identify experiences that develop the capabilities important to the organization

- stimulate reflection about memorable experiences that have taught critically important lessons about leadership and management

- provoke in-depth conversations about how to become an effective leader and manager

- give themselves and others the means to reflect on how they learn and how they approach situations that call for new learning

- create bonds of camaraderie in teams and between groups of people

- strengthen connections between senior, mid-level, and junior professionals and among people from different cultural backgrounds

- spark engagement and enthusiasm with team members and others

- facilitate social interactions at a networking event

When Can It Be Used?

Experience Explorer fits a variety of situations. It can be used in small-group workshops focused exclusively on experiences and lessons or as a short activity in a longer, broader, training-and-development class.

Different Places, Different Lessons

The lesson that matters the most to senior executives in Singapore, China, the U.S., and India is *managing direct reports or subordinates*. Among other top lessons learned are *self-awareness, executing effectively,* and *integrity*. *Executing effectively* is not among the top lessons in the U.S., and *integrity* is among the top three lessons in Singapore, China, and the U.S. but not India. India is unique in reporting *confidence* as the second most important lesson learned by its senior executives.

For example, Experience Explorer can be used when an organization wants to document and analyze the experiences that most effectively develop the leadership skills required in different roles, across functions and geographies. With that information, organizations can customize talent development.

On a smaller scale, Experience Explorer can be used when leaders want to share their experiences with peers, direct reports, and others as a way to coach how lessons learned translate into strategic career plans and lead to more effective leadership.

Who Can Conduct a Session?

Most people—managers, team leaders, trainers, facilitators, human-resource professionals, or training-and-development consultants—can all conduct a basic 60- to 90-minute Experience Explorer session. In most cases, it's sufficient to follow the instructions in this guide and to provide some basic directions to the people attending the session. After the participants receive a few simple instructions, the activity practically runs itself.

Beyond this, the facilitator needs only basic content knowledge corresponding to the session's objectives. For example, if the objective of the session is to reflect on how bosses and superiors can be influenced, or crises can be managed, or a cross-cultural assignment can be handled successfully, then the facilitator must have foundational knowledge of influencing skills, crisis management, or effective cross-cultural management.

Conducting an Experience Explorer Session

There are four steps to conducting a complete and successful Experience Explorer session.

1. **Set objectives.** The intention of the session must be clear and well articulated. Choose one of two paths—the Experience Path or the Lesson Path—that best suits the intent of the exercise.

2. **Sort and select.** Provide instructions as each participant sorts the Experience Explorer cards and then selects one to three Experience or Lesson cards, based on instructions that have been fine-tuned to meet session objectives.

3. **Share.** Guide participants as they tell others about memories and insights. This enables participants to tap more deeply into significant personal experiences and leadership lessons that have emerged from sorting the deck.

4. **Strategize.** Assist participants as they consider how they might use the insights gained during the preceding steps to form a plan for improving their leadership capabilities.

Pre-Session Checklist and Preparation

-   Set aside a minimum of 60 minutes (90 to 180 minutes is preferred).

-   Collect information about the available space and seating arrangements.

-   Confirm the number of people participating in the session and obtain basic information about their backgrounds.

-   Develop a clear statement about why you are using Experience Explorer and how the session will benefit its participants.

-   Give each participant one box of Experience Explorer cards.

-   Provide note-taking materials to participants, if they do not already have them.

-   Ensure you have a way to project, post, or hand out instructions. This is especially important if you are working in groups of more than ten participants. In large groups, the voice of the facilitator might not carry enough, and in the absence of a way to project/post/hand out instructions, participants who are a step behind others might miss later instructions and repeatedly approach the facilitator for them. Projecting/posting/handing out the instructions makes it easier to handle such situations.

- Ensure you have a sufficient number of flip charts, markers, and similar material for capturing the key points of large- or small-group discussions. The amount of recording material depends on the number of subgroups that will be formed during the session.

- (Optional) Obtain knowledge about the client's overarching agenda. If the Experience Explorer session is part of a broader program or organizational initiative, what part does the Experience Explorer activity play and what does it contribute to the overall effort?

Step-by-Step Instructions

Set objectives. The intention of the session must be clear and well articulated. Objectives can include teaching participants to do the following:

- understand that by paying attention to their own and others' memorable experiences they can teach themselves important lessons about leadership

- focus on learning from the specific experiences that are highly relevant to success in their organizational context

- understand how to tap their experiences for lessons relevant to the three dimensions of leadership: the worlds of work, people, and self

- form a career-development plan that will prepare them to lead more effectively within the context of their own jobs, roles, and organizational requirements

From an organizational standpoint, participants could use the Lesson or the Experience cards to answer questions such as

- How can the organization help managers get the experiences they need to develop themselves?

- How can the organization improve the ability of managers to learn from experience?

- How can the organization embed experience-based development into its leader-development strategy?

- How can the organizational culture adapt to support experience-driven development?

To clarify the session's objectives, facilitators must make one key decision in advance: to adopt either the Experience Path or the Lesson Path. The choice determines which set of cards the participants sort first.

The Experience Path begins with session participants identifying memorable experiences that have shaped who they are today and then guides them to reflect on lessons learned from these experiences.

The Lesson Path begins with session participants identifying current capabilities and then reflecting on experiences that contributed to their developing these capabilities.

Although both paths end with the participant strategizing to obtain necessary experiences and skills, the process of sorting and sharing for each path feels quite different.

Experience Path

The Experience Path works well when the participant group is diverse. For example, if the participants are from different organizations, represent different functions, or work in different geographies, this diversity can lead to an engaging discussion because of the group members' variety of experiences. Also, if the session is of a general nature and is not focused on a specific competency model or framework, you can use the Experience cards to help identify experiences from which the participant has learned his or her most powerful leadership lessons.

Lesson Path

The Lesson Path works well if participants are from the same organization, work in teams, or belong to a single function. If the participant group has a widely accepted core competency or leadership-development model in place, the Lesson cards help identify demonstrated strengths or capabilities necessary for future success. Participants who know each other are better able to identify others' strengths and development needs. They can also share stories that led, or can lead, to the development of specific capabilities.

Best practices for setting objectives. As the initial users of Experience Explorer, we have learned by making mistakes and then making adjustments on seemingly small but vital details. We share these best practices in the hope that they will bring you up to speed on this tool and ensure the success of your session.

- Be very clear on whether you choose the Experience Path or the Lesson Path. Do not attempt to do both in a single session. Remember that ultimately both paths will lead to developmental plans.

Three Worlds of Lessons

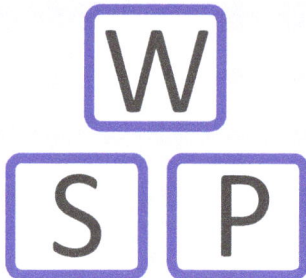

Leaders need balanced development and must learn lessons in three worlds, which are referred to in the cards as the World of Work, the World of People, and the World of Self. Surprisingly, participants in CCL programs often fail to recognize the importance of learning lessons that would help them to navigate through the worlds of people and self. But no one questions that leaders must learn lessons related to the world of work!

Sort and select. In this step, instruct participants to divide their cards based on the session objectives. Customize your instructions, depending on whether you have chosen the Experience Path or the Lesson Path (see Table 2).

Table 2. Sorting cards by path

The Experience Path	The Lesson Path
Say, "Please sort your cards into two stacks. Stack A has the experiences you have had, and stack B has the experiences you have not had."	Say, "Please sort your cards into two stacks. Stack A has the capabilities at which you are especially proficient, and stack B has the capabilities that you would like to develop or have been told to develop."

After sorting,

Say, "Set aside the cards describing experiences you have not had (stack B)."	Say, "Set aside the cards describing capabilities that you still have to develop (stack B)."

Instruct participants to select cards from the remaining deck (stack A).

Say, "Select one to three cards from the stack that remains. Choose the most memorable experiences that have shaped who you are as a leader."	Say, "Select one to three cards from the stack that remains. Choose capabilities of which you are especially proud."

Guide participants to reflect on the cards they have selected.

Say, "Think about the capabilities that you developed as a result of these experiences."	Say, "Think about the experiences that helped you to develop those capabilities."

Beyond your choice of the Experience Path or Lesson Path, you can further modify your instructions to meet the session's objectives. Table 3 contains examples of instructions to meet different objectives.

Table 3. Examples of sort instructions relative to session objectives

Objective	Say . . .
Create and manage change.	"Choose the most memorable experiences or lessons that taught you how to introduce and implement change."
Improve relationships with others.	"Choose the most memorable experiences or lessons from which you learned how to work effectively with others."
Increase self-awareness.	"Choose a powerful experience or lesson that taught you a great deal about your strengths and your limitations."
Learn from challenges at work.	"Choose one highly frustrating experience or lesson that taught you how to handle stress and become more resilient."
Improve learning agility.	"Choose a new or difficult experience or lesson from which you learned to handle an unfamiliar situation."
Identify future developmental experiences.	"Choose two or three job experiences that you would like to have in the next 3 to 18 months."
Build confidence.	"Choose an experience that made you very proud of what you or your team achieved."
Identify strengths through peer feedback.	"Choose one lesson that you see as a strength. (Ask the members in your group.)"

Best practices for sorting and selecting.

- You should circulate or display a copy of the step-by-step instructions/ questions for sorting. This will help participants who are behind the group to catch up without having to interrupt you for instructions.

- Be comfortable with the silence in the room when sorting takes place. Participants are going through an intense reflective journey and appreciate some time alone with their thoughts.

- Participants invest considerable time reflecting while they sort the cards into stacks. Ensure that the participants have enough space to keep four stacks separate, without tumbling over one another or getting their stacks mixed up with those of the next participant in the group.

For the Experience Path, participants will build four stacks:

1. Stack A: Experiences they have had (sort-and-select step).

2. Stack B: Experiences they have not had (sort-and-select step).

3. Stack C: Experience cards picked from stack B (strategize step).

4. Stack D: Lessons cards that indicate lessons they intend to learn from going through the experiences picked in stack C (strategize step).

For the Lesson Path, participants will build four stacks:

1. Stack A: Capabilities at which they are especially proficient (sort-and-select step).

2. Stack B: Capabilities that they would like to develop or have been told to develop (sort-and-select step).

3. Stack C: Lesson cards picked from stack B (strategize step).

4. Stack D: Experience cards that indicate experiences that they think will help them develop lessons identified in stack C (strategize step).

Share. In this step, participants share their memories and insights of past experiences or tell stories about capabilities at which they are proficient or would like to develop. This is done in pairs, small groups, or as a networking activity. Participants are reconvened as a large group to debrief the activity—including the sort-and-select step and the share step.

The instructions for sorting and selecting result in participants identifying cards that represent significant experiences in life or capabilities that are either strengths or weaknesses. Each participant may identify one or more cards for each case.

For sharing in the Experience Path, invite participants to talk in pairs or in small groups about their significant life experiences. Guide the other member or members of the group to probe for capabilities that were developed from the experiences being described.

When past experiences are selected, these are almost always loaded with mixed emotions. By describing their experience and the lessons they have learned from them—with one or more people, in a small group, or while mingling with many other people—participants revisit powerful events from their past. They are given an opportunity to have an open, honest conversation about a significant experience that has changed them in important ways. The conversation itself produces meaningful connections with others and is very empowering.

For sharing in the Lesson Path, invite participants to talk in pairs or in small groups about their demonstrated strengths. Guide the other member or members of the group to probe for experiences that led to the described capability being developed.

The Lesson cards represent leadership capabilities. When lessons are selected, participants come to grips with what they do well and where they need to improve themselves. Most find it satisfying to have clear knowledge about their strengths and limitations as leaders.

Following the exchange of stories, there is an abundance of insights in the room about the breadth of shared experiences and depth of lessons learned. Taking time to gather these insights deepens participants' understanding about how meaningful and engaging it is to tell others about their experiences and to listen to others tell their stories. Participants often remark on the considerable practical knowledge about effective leadership that the group holds.

Gather as many comments as you can in the time allotted. Record the comments so that the entire group can see them. You could show them on a screen, for example, or write them on a flip chart.

Best practices for sharing.

- Ensure that you provide adequate time for sharing among the participants. Be time conscious but do not rush through this step. A well-timed sharing session unlocks great value for participants. Typically, it takes a participant about 3 to 5 minutes to tell a story about an experience or lesson and what was learned from it. However, this time frame can vary by a number of factors, including culture, nationality, and organizational context. We have observed some sessions in which some participants took as long as 10 to 20 minutes to tell their stories.

- It is essential during the sharing step to be culturally sensitive. In some cultures, participants might be more comfortable sharing in larger groups rather than in pairs.

- Be flexible in order to stimulate conversation. Invite participants to talk one-on-one with the person next to them, to talk in small groups, or to circulate around the room and exchange experiences and lessons with as many people as possible.

- Make sure you tell participants how far they can spread out during conversations. You do not want people going off to the nearby café, for example, since getting them back into the room can be a challenge.

- Ensure that all group members share their thoughts; remind participants to take turns and not dominate the conversation.

- Ask the group questions to help stimulate conversation. For instance, you might ask:
    - Do you have any observations about sorting through the deck?
    - What did you notice about the stories you shared and heard?
    - What were the similarities and differences you heard among the stories?
    - What are your reactions and feelings about this activity?
    - What is positive about sharing experiences and lessons learned?

- How might the sharing of experiences and learned lessons have negative consequences?

- Share the data for the entire group. You can collect this data by inviting participants to put colored sticky dots on a listing of key experiences, by conducting a poll, or by calling for a show of hands.

- Keep in mind that different factors can influence the duration of this step. For example, consider the depth of conversational exchanges you want the tool to stimulate, the space in which you are conducting the session, and the seating arrangements.

Strategize. This step is transformative. It takes participants from a focus on past experiences and leadership lessons to a focus on desired capabilities and future experiences that can teach those capabilities.

We recommend that participants translate the insights they have gained into action plans for developing themselves or others. Ideally, you would start the action-planning process toward the end of the session. Thinking about "So now what?" aids people in reflecting on how they can go about pursuing specific experiences and lessons for developing themselves and others back in the workplace.

For example, participants could plan what experience they would want to take on next, or what skill they would want to develop in the next year, or both. As another example, if the focus of the session has been on lessons, participants could note the distribution of their skills among the three worlds of work, people, and self. Then they could strategize to develop those skills that will balance their professional and personal development by improving their capabilities in all three worlds.

Table 4 provides some suggestions on instructions for this step.

Table 4. Strategies for each path

The Experience Path	The Lesson Path
Say, "Now, pick up stack B (the card stack of 'Experiences that I have not had'). From this, select one or two cards that indicate the experiences that would most likely give a boost to your career."	Say, "Now, pick up stack B (the card stack of 'Capabilities that you would like to develop or have been told to develop'). From this, select three to eight cards that indicate the capabilities that you would most like to develop in order to be even more effective in your role."
Say, "Now select only one of these cards that represents the experience that you are most interested in—one that you are willing to target as a developmental goal."	Say, "Now select only one of these cards that represents the capability that you are most interested in developing—one that you are willing to target as a developmental goal."
Say, "Note down a realistic time frame over which you would like to have this experience. Research tells us that a time frame of at least 6 months to 2 years makes the most sense."	Say, "Note down a realistic time frame over which you would like to acquire this new capability. Research tells us that a time frame of at least a month to at most a year makes the most sense."
Say, "From the orange Lesson cards, list the new knowledge, skills, perspectives, or behaviors that you expect to acquire through this experience."	Say, "List the new knowledge, skills, perspectives, or behaviors that you will need to cultivate in yourself to acquire this capability."
	Say, "Identify two to five experiences or activities—at work or outside work—that could help you to develop this capability and meet the goal you have set for yourself."

For both paths, here are some common instructions that can be used:

- Say, "Write down the names of people you can turn to for guidance— such as bosses, mentors, peers, subordinates, friends, family, and teachers."
- Say, "What other resources or practices could be helpful to you?"
- Say, "What do you see as the best benefits to you of developing this new capability or having this new experience?"

Best practices for strategizing.

- Ensure you have adequate time for this step, since it represents what the participants take back from the session and can act on immediately.
- If your session is sponsored by an organization for an existing group, align your activity with existing organizational frameworks and tools.
- When closing the session, ensure that every set of cards is complete.

Options and Applications

In this section you will learn some of the different ways in which facilitators of Experience Explorer have used the tool and different options for some of the steps.

Sort Option 1: Sorting the Categories of Experiences

Each Experience card is marked with a dot in the lower-right corner. The color of the dot corresponds to one of the five main categories of developmental experiences that the fifteen core leadership experiences fall into: challenging assignments, developmental relationships, coursework & training, hardships, and personal life experiences (see Table 5).

These categories represent five broad sources of leader development—each with different learning dynamics. For example, learning from a challenging assignment involves engaging in action to solve problems and accomplish tasks, and then generating knowledge and insights from seeing the consequences of those actions. Learning from developmental relationships involves observing, seeking advice and support, engaging in dialogue, and receiving feedback. Learning from hardships often happens primarily after the experience when the individual reflects on and seeks to make sense of the hardship.

The dots marking the Experience cards can be used in a variety of ways:

- **You can examine differences in experiences that a person has had and not had.** Ask participants to notice the categories of experiences they have had or not had. Are the experiences related to each category (for example, challenging assignments, developmental relationships) equally distributed across the "have had" and "not had" stacks, or is there a category or two where almost all the experiences are in the "not had" stack? What might this say about the kinds of experience one naturally seeks out?

We encourage every user to share their experiences, tips, solutions, ideas, and adaptations by visiting www.ccl.org/Explorer.

Table 5. Categories of experiences

	Experience Category (number of cards of this type in deck)	Experience Types (number of cards of this type in deck)
● Orange	Challenging Assignments (26)	Cultural Crossing (4) Horizontal Move (5) Increase in Job Scope (4) New Initiative (4) Stakeholder Engagement (6) Turnaround/Fix-it (3)
● Pink	Developmental Relationships (12)	Bosses & Superiors (4) Difficult People (3) Feedback & Coaching (5)
● Yellow	Coursework & Training (3)	Coursework & Training (3)
● Teal	Hardships (9)	Career Setback (2) Crisis (5) Ethical Dilemma (1) Mistake (1)
● Red	Personal Life Experiences (2)	Personal Experience (2)

- **You can examine how learning varies in different kinds of experiences.** Ask participants to divide their "have had" cards by the colored dots. How was learning different when experiencing a challenging assignment compared to a developmental relationship, a course, a hardship, or a personal life experience? What does it take to learn effectively from each of these sources?

- **You can illustrate 70-20-10.** Three of the categories match with the 70-20-10 guideline for leadership development. This guideline suggests that a combination of 70% challenging assignments, 20% developmental relationships, and 10% coursework is optimal for preparing managers for leadership roles. Participants can examine the distribution of the experiences that they have had to see how closely it reflects this guideline.

- **You can emphasize the central role of challenging assignments.** Because a major portion of leadership development happens as a result of challenging assignments, facilitators may want to focus specifically on this category of experiences. For example, the challenging assignments cards could be pulled out and serve as the basis for the entire exercise. Or in the strategize step, an emphasis could be placed on seeking "orange dot" experiences.

Did You Know?

Although the five main categories of developmental experiences are consistent across countries, there are two more experiences that, when all are combined, are the source of 70% to 80% of all leadership lessons learned by executives from that country. These additional experiences are different from country to country. To illustrate, *personal experience* tops the list in India but *mistakes* are among the most frequently mentioned experience in China and the U.S., and *stakeholder engagement* is the one most frequently cited by Singapore's public-sector leaders. CCL research continues its pursuit to explain why these differences occur.

Sort Option 2: Sorting the Worlds of Lessons

Each Lesson card is marked with a symbol in the lower-right corner. This symbol indicates which of the three dimensions of lessons each card falls into: World of Work, World of People, and World of Self (see Table 6).

Table 6. Dimensions of lessons

	Category (number of cards of this type in deck)	Definition of Category
W	World of Work (15)	Lessons cards having this symbol represent capabilities that are related to getting work done.
P	World of People (15)	Lessons cards having this symbol represent capabilities that are related to interpersonal relationships.
S	World of Self (12)	Lessons cards having this symbol represent capabilities that are related to leading and managing oneself as a leader.

These categories represent three worlds of lessons or capabilities that leaders must develop. Leaders need to develop capabilities to get work done (World of Work). Even as they get work done, leaders need to manage and develop interpersonal relationships all around them, such as with superiors, supervisors, peers, direct reports, and external stakeholders (World of People). And, as they get the work done in relationship with others, leaders need to attend to their own development from a career and a personal perspective (World of Self).

The world categories can be used in a variety of ways:

- **You can examine current capabilities.** Ask participants to notice which worlds their current capabilities fall in. Are all their capabilities in just one world (for example, the World of Work)? What impact might this have on their ability to advance in their careers and meet demands of future roles?

- **You can examine current areas for development.** Ask participants to notice which world capabilities they aspire to develop or have been told to develop. What might support or hinder their ability to develop capability in these worlds?

- **You can emphasize the need to develop all three worlds of capabilities.** Ask participants to sort the Lesson cards into three stacks that represent the three worlds of capabilities. Next, for the first world stack (for example, World of Work), ask participants to separate the cards into two stacks: "strengths" and "needs development." Repeat the process with the other world stacks. Participants can then come up with a table like the one in Table 7 below and use it to approach their development plans strategically.

Table 7. Sorting lessons by strengths and developmental needs

World of Work		World of People		World of Self	
Strengths	Needs Development	Strengths	Needs Development	Strengths	Needs Development
planning and execution problem solving	risk-taking initiating/ managing change	building/ managing a team gaining respect and influence	managing external stakeholders dealing with conflict	being humane/ empathic adaptability/ flexibility	confidence self-awareness

Application 1: Life Coaching

Reviewing and reflecting on recent experiences is important to gaining clarity about the direction a person wants to take in his or her life. Experience Explorer gives both people in a life-coaching session (usually a one-on-one coaching or mentoring session) an opportunity to immediately share ideas, thoughts, and feelings within a structure that encourages open conversation.

Facilitation. Follow the instructions for conducting a basic session. Ask the person being coached to sort the Experience cards and then share his or her memories and reactions to the cards.

Application benefits. Using Experience Explorer in this low-risk way can help leaders and managers—or, for that matter, anyone in a formal or informal coaching relationship—make quick progress on some of their development needs. The tool does not require deep analysis. Instead, the coach and the coachee can simply observe the facts of experience. Awareness leads to actions, self-confidence, and perspective—accelerating development as the coachee steps away from murky memories and vague life goals.

Additional resources. The following resources can be helpful in this application:

King, S. N., Altman, D. G., & Lee, R.J. (2011). *Discovering the leader in you: How to realize your leadership potential* (new and rev. ed.). San Francisco, CA: Jossey-Bass.

King, S. N., & Altman, D. G. (2011). *Discovering the leader in you workbook*. San Francisco, CA: Jossey-Bass.

Wei, R., & Yip, J. (2008). *Leadership wisdom: Discovering the lessons of experience.* Greensboro, NC: Center for Creative Leadership.

Application 2: Career Planning

Career advancement does not always follow a straight or an obvious path. Use Experience Explorer with an early- or mid-career manager who is ready for a career transition and needs help thinking about the next move.

Facilitation. The manager looking for his or her next career move should take ownership of the session. Hand the manager the Experience Explorer cards. Ask the manager to select some of his or her most important experiences and to identify the lessons learned from each of those experiences.

During the session, patterns will emerge as to the kinds of experiences and lessons the manager has had and what was learned from them. It will also become clear to the manager what kinds of experiences he or she has not had. For example, a manager might lack start-up experience or might never have handled a crisis.

At this point, it only takes a few questions from the facilitator to help the manager clearly see what is needed from his or her next assignment. When presented a range of options, the manager will have criteria for evaluating the benefits of job assignments.

Application benefits. Experience Explorer puts a person's development squarely in his or her own hands. By assuming an equal share of the conversation, managers see for themselves the potential gaps in their development. Experience Explorer goes a long way in helping managers be rigorous and intentional about planning career progression.

Additional resources. The following resources can be helpful in this application:

Chappelow, C. T., & Leslie, J. B. (2001). *Keeping your career on track: Twenty success strategies*. Greensboro, NC: Center for Creative Leadership.

McCauley, C. D. (2006). *Developmental assignments: Creating learning experiences without changing jobs*. Greensboro, NC: Center for Creative Leadership.

McCauley, C. D., DeRue, S. D., Yost, P. R., & Taylor, S. (2014). *Experience-driven leader development: Models, tools, best practices, and advice for on-the-job development*. San Francisco, CA: Wiley.

McCauley, C. D., & Martineau, J. W. (1998). *Reaching your development goals*. Greensboro, NC: Center for Creative Leadership.

Van Velsor, E. (2013). *Broadening your organizational perspective*. Greensboro, NC: Center for Creative Leadership.

Wilson, M. S. (2010). *Developing tomorrow's leaders today: Insights from corporate India*. Singapore: Wiley.

Application 3: Resilience and Learning Agility

Experience Explorer has been an effective tool for assisting mid-career executives and others learn to be more resilient and open to learning in the face of new or difficult experiences.

Facilitation. Facilitation is a two-part event. First, use Experience Explorer to introduce participants to one another. After asking them to select a memorable experience, ask participants to select the most significant lesson that shaped them as leaders. Using the basic instructions for sharing, members of the group quickly become familiar with one another.

In the second phase, link the ideas of learning agility to the topic of resilience. This is done by setting the stage with a personal story that illustrates how resilience and learning agility in the face of difficult assignments are two sides of the same coin. Then use the experience cards in the usual way, guiding participants to select experiences that have demonstrated their ability to be resilient. The connection between resilience and personal growth and development becomes clear very quickly. Participants come away with an appreciation for how resilience helps them not just to bounce back from challenges and survive but to engage challenges and thrive.

Whenever possible, invite top and senior leaders to attend the second phase of the session and share their own most important lessons and memorable experiences.

Application benefits. When learning becomes more intentional, as it does during an Experience Explorer session, participants grasp how they can combine their preferred learning style with their capacity of resilience. The idea that difficult challenges are opportunities and not obstacles can become even clearer to the group if the organization's senior leaders describe how they navigated their experiences and learned from them.

Additional resources. The following resources can be helpful in this application:

Bunker, K. A. (2008). *Responses to change: Helping people manage transition.* Greensboro, NC: Center for Creative Leadership.

Dalton, M. (1998). *Becoming a more versatile learner.* Greensboro, NC: Center for Creative Leadership.

Pulley, M. L., & Wakefield, M. (2001). *Building resiliency: How to thrive in times of change*. Greensboro, NC: Center for Creative Leadership.

Ruderman, M. N., & Ohlott, P. J. (2001). *Learning from life: Turning life's lessons into leadership experience*. Greensboro, NC: Center for Creative Leadership.

Wei, R. R., & Yip, J. (2008). *Leadership wisdom: Discovering the lessons of experience*. Greensboro, NC: Center for Creative Leadership.

Wilson, M. S. (2010). *Developing tomorrow's leaders today: Insights from corporate India*. Singapore: Wiley.

Introduction

Using Experience Explorer

Conducting an Experience Explorer Session

Options and Applications

References and Resources

Research Background

About the Authors

References and Resources

Bunker, K. A. (2008). *Responses to change: Helping people manage transition*. Greensboro, NC: Center for Creative Leadership.

Chappelow, C. T., & Leslie, J. B. (2001). *Keeping your career on track: Twenty success strategies*. Greensboro, NC: Center for Creative Leadership.

Dalton, M. (1998). *Becoming a more versatile learner*. Greensboro, NC: Center for Creative Leadership.

Douglas, C. (2003). *Key events and lessons for managers in a diverse workforce*. Greensboro, NC: Center for Creative Leadership.

King, S. N., Altman, D. G., & Lee, R. J. (2011). *Discovering the leader in you: How to realize your leadership potential* (new and rev. ed.). San Francisco, CA: Jossey-Bass.

King, S. N., & Altman, D. G. (2011). *Discovering the leader in you workbook*. San Francisco, CA: Jossey-Bass.

McCall, M. W., Jr. (1998). *High flyers: Developing the next generation of leaders*. Boston, MA: Harvard Business School Press.

McCall, M. W., Jr., & Hollenbeck, G. P. (2002). *Developing global executives: The lessons of international experience*. Boston, MA: Harvard Business School Press.

McCall, M. W., Jr., Lombardo, M. M., & Morrison, A. M. (1988). *The lessons of experience: How successful executives develop on the job*. Lexington, MA: Lexington Books.

McCauley, C. D. (2006). *Developmental assignments: Creating learning experiences without changing jobs*. Greensboro, NC: Center for Creative Leadership.

McCauley, C. D., DeRue, S. D., Yost, P. R., & Taylor, S. (2014). *Experience-driven leader development: Models, tools, best practices, and advice for on-the-job development*. San Francisco, CA: Wiley.

McCauley, C. D., & Martineau, J. W. (1998). *Reaching your development goals*. Greensboro, NC: Center for Creative Leadership.

McCauley, C. D., Ohlott, P. J., & Ruderman, M. N. (1999). *The job challenge profile facilitator's guide*. Greensboro, NC: Center for Creative Leadership.

McCauley, C. D., Ruderman, M. N., & Ohlott, P. J. (1994). Assessing the developmental components of managerial jobs. *Journal of Applied Psychology, 79*(4), 544–560.

Morrison, A., White, R., & Van Velsor, E. (1987). *Breaking the glass ceiling: Can women make it to the top of America's biggest corporations?* Reading, MA: Addison Wesley.

Moxley, R., & Pulley, M. (2004). Learning from hardships. In C. D. McCauley & E. Van Velsor (Eds.), *The Center for Creative Leadership handbook of leadership development* (2nd ed., pp. 183–203). San Francisco, CA: Jossey-Bass.

Pulley, M. L., & Wakefield, M. (2001). *Building resiliency: How to thrive in times of change*. Greensboro, NC : Center for Creative Leadership.

Ruderman, M., & Ohlott, P. J. (2001). *Learning from life: Turning life's lessons into leadership experience*. Greensboro, NC: Center for Creative Leadership.

Scisco, P., McCauley, C. D., Leslie, J. B., & Elsey, R. (2014). *Change now: Five steps to better leadership*. Greensboro, NC: Center for Creative Leadership.

Van Velsor, E. (2013). *Broadening your organizational perspective*. Greensboro, NC: Center for Creative Leadership.

Van Velsor, E., Criswell, C., Puryear, K., & Hollenbeck, N. (2011). *Learning leadership in the military: Key developmental events and lessons from senior military officers*. Greensboro, NC: Center for Creative Leadership.

Van Velsor, E., Wilson, M., Criswell, C., & Chandrasekar, A. (2013). Learning to lead: A comparison of developmental events and learning. *Asian Business and Management Special Issue on Leadership Development and Global Talent Management in the Asian Context*, 455–476.

Wei, R., & Yip, J. (2008). *Leadership wisdom: Discovering the lessons of experience*. Greensboro, NC: Center for Creative Leadership.

Wilson, M. S. (2010). *Developing tomorrow's leaders today: Insights from corporate India*. Singapore: Wiley.

Wilson, M. S., & Hoole, E. (2011). Developing leadership: India at the crossroads. *Vikalpa: The Journal for Decision Makers, 36*(3), 1–8. Ahmedabad, India: Indian Institute of Management.

Wilson, M. S., & Van Velsor, E. (2010). The new terrain of leadership development. In S. Verma (Ed.), *Toward the next orbit: A corporate odyssey* (pp. 269–284). New Delhi, India: Sage.

Yip, J., & Wilson, M. S. (2008). *Developing public service leaders in Singapore*. (Technical report). Greensboro, NC: Center for Creative Leadership.

Zhang, Y., Chandrasekar, A., & Wei, R. (2009). *Developing future leaders for Chinese companies*. (Technical report). Greensboro, NC: Center for Creative Leadership.

Research Background: The Lessons of Experience

CCL's research into the lessons that executives learn from experience has spanned a number of years, countries, and organizational types (see Figure 4 below), and it has generated many practical results. The suite of studies, for example, resulted in a training program specifically designed for human-resources managers (*Assessment Certification Workshop*) and classroom exercises for several other leader development programs. Two other assessments came out of the research: *Benchmarks* and *Job Challenge Profile*.

The research also launched several books and many articles. Most recently, *Developing Tomorrow's Leaders Today: Insights from Corporate India* (2010) and a white paper, *Grooming Top Leaders: Cultural Perspectives from China, India, Singapore, and the United States* (2011). Researchers from around the world continue to adapt and use the methodology from the research on the lessons of experience and release their own academic and popular articles and presentations.

Figure 4. The history of CCL's Lessons of Experience research

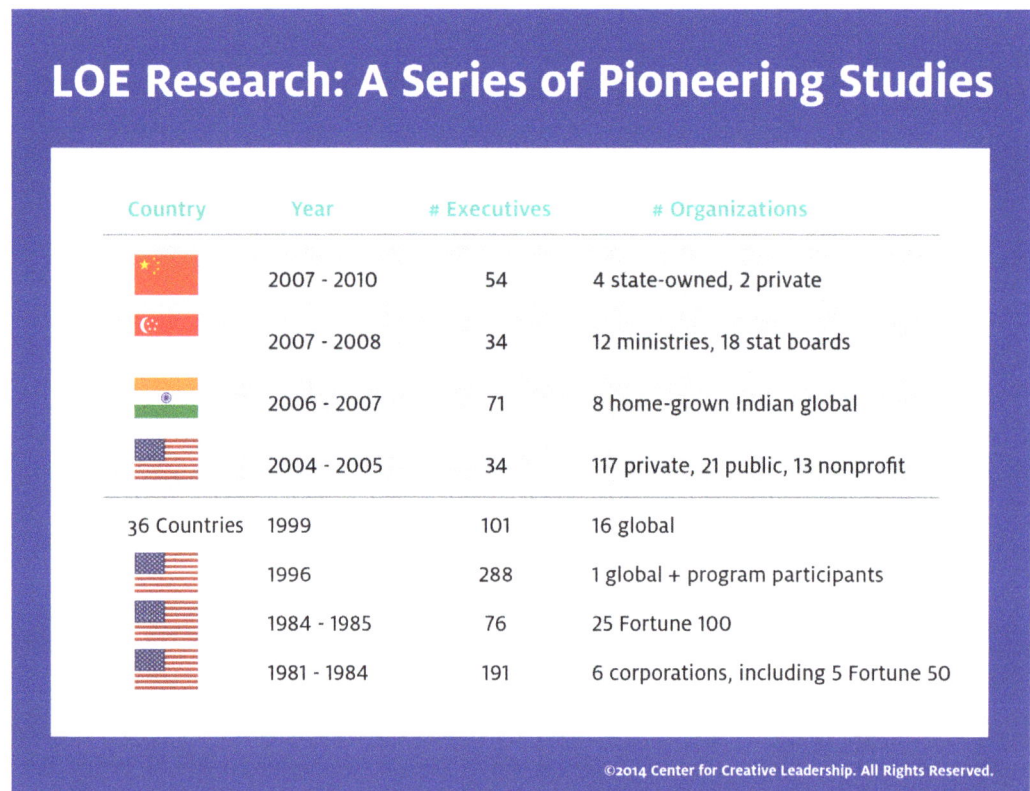

LOE Research: A Series of Pioneering Studies

Country	Year	# Executives	# Organizations
China	2007 - 2010	54	4 state-owned, 2 private
Singapore	2007 - 2008	34	12 ministries, 18 stat boards
India	2006 - 2007	71	8 home-grown Indian global
USA	2004 - 2005	34	117 private, 21 public, 13 nonprofit
36 Countries	1999	101	16 global
USA	1996	288	1 global + program participants
USA	1984 - 1985	76	25 Fortune 100
USA	1981 - 1984	191	6 corporations, including 5 Fortune 50

©2014 Center for Creative Leadership. All Rights Reserved.

About the Authors

Meena S. Wilson is a senior enterprise associate at CCL and author of *Developing Tomorrow's Leaders Today: Insights from Corporate India* (Wiley, 2010), which is based on in-depth interviews with over a hundred senior executives from eight global Indian companies.

A dedicated and versatile professional, Meena has led several significant start-ups during her 20 years at CCL. She opened the APAC campus in Singapore as interim managing director (2003) and later launched a Singapore-based research, innovation, and product development unit (2006). Meena also served as principal investigator for the *Lessons of Experience-Asia* project, managing cross-organizational teams in India, Singapore, and China (2009). She is now based in Gurgaon and Jamshedpur with responsibilities for developing regionally useful products, services, and client solutions.

Meena is committed to promoting cutting-edge leadership-development practices, and she continues her research on accelerating top-talent development, advancing women's careers, and improving cross-cultural effectiveness.

N. Anand Chandraseker is a senior research faculty member at CCL and is a lead developer of the *Leadership Gap Indicator* assessment, which provides organizations with a tool for evaluating managers' opinions about development needs.

Presently based in Singapore, Anand combines the rigor of academia with a practical approach to research and then translates the resulting knowledge into solutions that provide sustained impact on individuals, businesses, and the world. Anand has authored peer-reviewed academic journals, book chapters, research reports, white papers, and newspaper articles. His research interests lie at the intersection of three broad domains: leadership development, positive psychology, and Indian psychology. His current research is aimed at understanding the relationship of generosity and leadership.

Start a creative conversation

When collaborative conversations need to occur around a variety of leadership issues, CCL's portfolio of Leadership Explorer™ tools will help pave the way. These visual and tactile tools can address a wide variety of situations to help develop ideas and insights into useful dialogue. Our Leadership Explorer tools are based on decades of cutting-edge research and time-tested experience with thousands of individuals from around the world.

Leadership Explorer Tools

Visual Explorer™ opens creative conversations and deep dialogues – using a wide variety of images – about almost any topic chosen by the user.

Leadership Metaphor Explorer™ uses drawings and captions to increase understanding of how leadership operates in organizations, communities, and across boundaries.

Experience Explorer™ helps leaders to reflect on their most memorable workplace experiences, and what they learned about leadership and management from each experience.

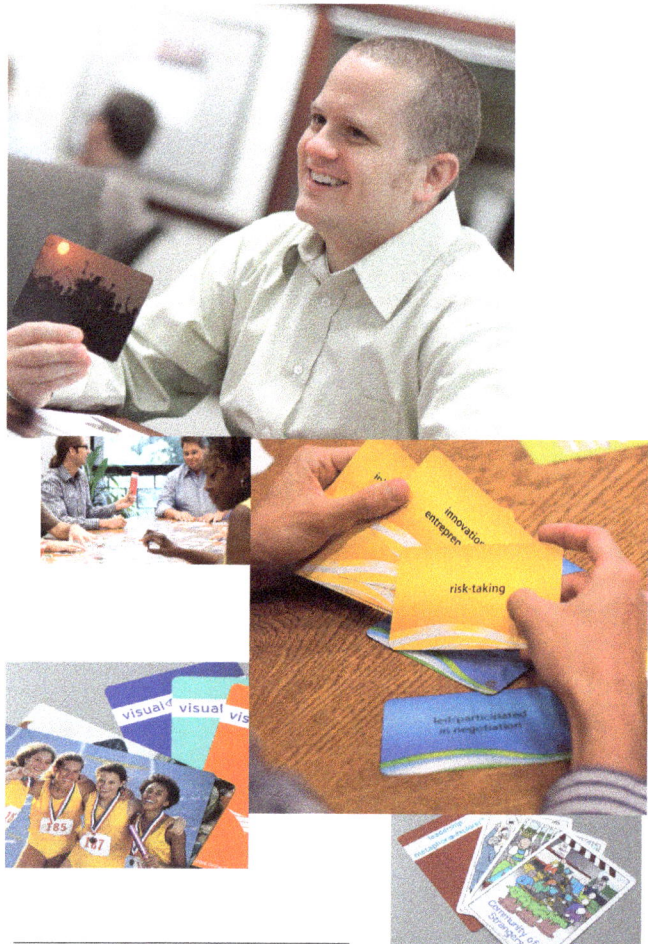

Other Explorer tools are offered as beta versions by CCL Labs for further user testing and feedback.

Values Explorer™ helps create a structured conversation that surfaces values for self and mutual understanding, prioritizing, and planning.

Boundary Explorer™ is a teaching aid and planning tool that explores strategies and tactics for spanning boundaries and creating new frontiers for innovation.

Wisdom Explorer™ features wisdom quotations drawn from around the globe and across the ages, and puts them into the middle of a creative conversation.

Center for Creative Leadership®

For more information on these tools visit www.ccl.org/explorer call + 1 336 545 2810 or email info@ccl.org

www.ingramcontent.com/pod-product-compliance
Lightning Source LLC
Chambersburg PA
CBHW051659210326
41518CB00025B/2605